LAW AND ORDER
IN CAERNARFON

Law and Order
in Caernarfon

Margaret Hughes

First published in 2007

© Text: Margaret Hughes

ISBN: 1-84524-063-4
978-1-84524-063-9

Cover design: Sian Parri

First published in 2007 by
Llygad Gwalch, Ysgubor Plas, Llwyndyrys,
Pwllheli, Gwynedd LL53 6NG
☎ 01758 750432   🖷 01758 750438
✆ gai@llygadgwalch.com   Web site: www.carreg-gwalch.co.uk

Contents

Acknowledgments . . .

'Law and Order in Caernarfon' would not have been written without valuable help from many people. After incorporating their advice and expertise I readily admit that should there be any errors in the text, they are mine alone.

Ann Rhydderch and her staff at the Gwynedd County Record Office have given patient and efficient attention to my enquiries over many visits. Mrs Rhydderch, as secretary of the Caernarfonshire Historical Society, has also given permission to quote from the Society's Transactions.

Beryl Evans, South Reading Room Manager, Department of Public Services at the National Library of Wales, gave guidance towards available sources at Aberystwyth. Also, the Librarian/Archivist at NCCL Galleries of Justice, Nottingham, allowed permission to quote from several Prison Reports and also the findings of the investigation into the behaviour of two Victorian prison governors. I am greatly indebted to Nick Tucker, for his generous work in tracing sources.

Joe Large, Usher at Caernarfon Crown Court; Margaret Hemmings, OBE, JP, and John Rowlands, OBE, carefully directed me through the complexities – and changes – of court procedures over the years.

T. Meirion Hughes, Resident Historian of the Caernarfon Royal Town Council, has shown great interest and has kindly allowed me to quote from his work.

I am grateful to them all . . . and, as ever, to Gwasg Carreg Gwalch, not only for the commission to research and write on such an absorbing topic, but for their ever-pleasant co-operation through all the stages of publication, and for providing illustrations.

Margaret Hughes
Llanfairpwll 2006

Introduction

'Law and Order in Caernarfon' is a taster, a brief picture of how the law has been administered in the town over the centuries. It is not an exhaustive study. The subject is too vast. It would need extensive research, and would fill a volume far larger than this.

The contents have been gleaned from official sources and from the personal comment of those who have written and spoken of their experiences.

Petty Sessions, Quarter Sessions and Assizes have all been held in Caernarfon. Justices of the Peace have played a prominent part over the years since the office was first introduced by Henry VIII in 1536. This book deals mainly with the business of the Quarter Sessions in which Justices of the Peace featured so prominently.

Caernarfon's law and order records since the 16th century are the second most comprehensive still extant in Britain. Assize records are at the Public Record Office at Kew. Petty and Quarter Sessions papers can be seen at the Gwynedd County Record Office in Caernarfon.

The reader will be able to compare the nature of crime over the years, and reflect how they mirror the social conditions of the times in north-west Wales when they were committed.

The Background

Before the Statute of Rhuddlan, 1284 (or, as sometimes called, the Statute of Wales) which marked the end of the medieval period in Welsh history, the administration of law and order in Wales was arbitrary, following mainly the laws of Hywel Dda who had died some three and a half centuries earlier. A number of courts operated, most of them based on the geographical divisions of hundreds and commotes. These attempted to deal with a variety of cases. There were also manorial and other private courts. Church courts handled ecclesiastical matters. A small civil court was held every three weeks in Caernarfon to hear cases of debt and slander. The Piepowder court sat during fair days to hear disputes between buyers and sellers whose stay in the town was temporary. The Sheriff was in charge of both.

Policing as we know it today was non-existent until the 19th century. Charges were made by individuals upon other individuals, who were brought to court with the help of a bailiff, or a constable of Caernarfon castle.

Edward I, by his Statute, introduced the English legal system to Wales. Shires or counties were formed – Caernarfonshire was one of three in northern Wales. Each had its own Sheriff and county court. Every one of the courts in the county network worked similarly, and became the basis of present-day administration of law and order.

Towns flourished around Edward's castles. They became the natural centres for commerce. Carnarvon (so spelled in documents of the day) had long since been a small port, but on the completion of the castle and because of its consequent elevation in status in the area, the port soon became an important commercial and administrative centre of the new shire.

Rules were laid down whereby burgesses of Caernarfon were restricted to selling goods within their own markets. The town grew in importance as trade flourished and the effects of the Statute of Rhuddlan were experienced.

Caernarfon castle, huge though it was, was never manned to capacity. Constables of the castle were important in its staffing. Four were elected annually and had to swear allegiance on oath which also underlined their responsibilities in the maintenance of order. They were charged:

You shall well and truly serve our Sovereign Lord the King in the Office of Constable to and for the Town and liberties of Carnarvon for the year ensuing and untill you of your said office be Discharged by due course of law. You shall see that His Majesty's peace be kept to the utmost of your power. You shall arrest and take all such persons as you shall find comitting any Riotts Debates or Affrays. You shall to the Utmost of your power endeavour that the Statute of Windsor for Disorderly persons be putt in Execution within this Town and liberties upon complaint to you made, you shall endeavour to apprehend all ffelons Riotous persons, Affray makers, and if any Offenders in this kind shall make any resistance you shall follow after them, with Hue and Cry untill they be taken. You shall be obedient to the Mayor and Bayliffs of this Town, and also you shall execute all proofs and precepts, mandetts and warrants to you directed and delivered. You shall also true presentiment make of all Blood shedders and other misdemeaners and truly do and execute to all things belonging thereunto according to ye best of yr. understanding. (So help you God)

Constables were unpaid. Although the office held a certain cachet it was not popular with the holders as the time spent precluded working to maintain their homes and families and, often, their business.

Sheriffs were appointed by the Crown for one year. Their main duty was financial but they did sit at the county court, at the hundred court for pleas under forty shillings and at the biennial tourns and the Piepowder court. During this period the Mayor and Bailiffs had some jurisdiction in matters of assault, 'blood drawing' as well as having 'the privilege of the gallows', this being the right to hang thieves taken within the town walls. The Caernarfon gallows was outside the town, near Pont Seiont, until some years later when executions were carried out in the Dungeon Tower of the town wall which was then part of the Gaol.

Although an improvement on the old arbitrary courts, the new legal system had its problems. These were eventually ironed out with yet another important reform, created by Henry VIII who, in 1536, introduced a new tier of justice by creating the office of Justice of the Peace and a new court framework.

The 1536 Act called for eight magistrates (Justices of the Peace) to be appointed for each county, a number raised in time to at least twenty. All were to be chosen from the gentry.

Quarter Sessions courts were held four times a year before a Justice and a Recorder. The Quarter Sessions tried misdemeanours and summary cases. Felonies, now called indictable offences, were usually heard before a judge at Assizes, held twice a year.

Friday, September 30, 1541, was an important day at Caernarfon. This was the date of the first Quarter Sessions meeting held in the town, when Sir Richard Bulkeley and other Justices attended. One of their first convictions was to hang a man for stealing five 'carrfuls' of hay valued at twenty pence. This case did not go to the Assize court. The first Quarter Sessions meeting was held in one of the town's many public houses.

Each Sessions day would attract crowds from the surrounding countryside, all keen to see the gentry arriving. Around the site of the present Shire Hall there would be a throng of sightseers, traders, vagabonds out for useful pickings, but all to stare at the important arrivals. Assizes proved to be the most colourful, with the judge in his robes of office.

Until medieval times the gentry had wielded considerable control over administering Wales, so they were the natural choice for this important new office of Justice of the Peace. They had to be able to converse in and understand English. The Grand Jury for Assizes was chosen from the lesser gentry.

If Justices failed to appear at a court for any reason, they were fined.

From the start, records of both Quarter Sessions and Assizes in Caernarfon are full. They reflect society in all its guises from the middle of the 16th century to modern times.

Quarter Sessions records, originally in Latin, have been translated by the late W. Ogwen Williams. They make fascinating reading. The calendar of Quarter Sessions papers at the Gwynedd County Record Office makes access to the many hundreds of official papers simple.

The Justices' workload

The introduction of the new legal class of Justice of the Peace brought a radical change to the way law and order, in its widest sense, was accomplished. Not only did the appointed officers have to deal with crime but they were also expected to act as what we, today, would term local government officers. This persisted from the days of Henry VIII until the Local Government Act of 1835, when local government received the framework upon which it operates today.

There were many problems needing the attention of the Justices, especially so in the important town of Caernarfon. The 17th century saw a variety of problems presented in the same court. One 'presentment' to the Justices read:

> Wee of the towne Jury doe present the owners of the dunghills lying on the greene called Maceyllase. Lyquise wee presente the ffludgate or sluse on the midle of the greate bridge leding into the towne. Lyquise wee present Richard Will' Morris for his Lyme Pitts. Wee also present That Robert ap Hugh Gwynn of Llanbeblick, gent', this pr'sent day in our heareing did sweare six othes by God woundes and blod he being playing crosse and pile.

Justices of Caernarfon court dealt with cases from all over the county. In 1623 they heard a complaint from the postmaster at Beaumaris who wanted clearer and safer access for mail over the Lavan Sands. Part of the sands, on the mainland side, were within Caernarfonshire:

The humble peticon of Rowland ap Robert Postm'r of Bewmares in ye Countie of Anglesey . . . To the honourable S'r Peeter Mutton kt. and Mr Nettleton, Justices of Assise in North Wales . . . most humbly sheweth that y'our peticoner and his servantes have been ymploied these 11 years and above in carrying his Ma'ties packettes to Conway and in guardinge noblemen & gentlemen strangers that rid for his Ma'ties affaires by post that way. And many times when sudden mistes and foggs doe fall. The danger is very great uppon the sandes that ye Kinges packettes and subjectes are like to perish wch moved me about four years past to be an humble peticoner to the then Judges of Assise in these p'tes that they would be pleased to give order that at everymile end of the sandes, a maine poste might be fixed, and every quarter of a mile smaller stakes that may guide such of his Ma'ties subjects as have cause to travel that way which they were pleased to graunt and give their pr'sent order to certaine gentlemen of Carnarvonshire to see it p'formed but as yet it is not donne.

There were similar disputes, over many years, concerning the upkeep of roads and bridges in the county.

Justices of the Peace were expected to regulate alehouses and inns. In 1634 there were fifty-seven alehouses in the town, thirty of them not licensed. Central government, during the days of the Commonwealth, moved to deal positively with these miscreants. It was part of the new official moral code of the Puritans who also frowned upon heavy drinking and sabbath-breaking. Vagabonds and beggars received short shrift as they were dragged before their betters. Harry Owen, in 1631, was one of these:

Your enformer enformeth your Wor' that the said Harry Owen is a common hunter of alehouses, a player at dice and cards both for money and ale and that he useth to play under hedges where he meets his companions both for money, sheep, hennes and clothes . . . the said defendt. useth to goe in other mens names to mercers and taketh up from theire shoppes certain commodities and wares unknown to the parties.

Characters indeed! Harry was also accused of being a sheep stealer and 'a puller of sheepes wolle'.

Commercial cheating took place widely throughout the centuries, and had to be kept well under control in the important trading centre of Caernarfon, as we are reminded by an early record:

Roger Llo'd for forstallying of the Kynges markyt in bying of fyshe at the Weyres at Llanvagelan octo salmones for the price of viujd and selling the same at Carnarvon for xijd . . . the same Roger for reilying and miskallying the quest salmorum to the great injury of the said borough.

Country traditions, which had become unofficial laws with the passage of time, had to be maintained:

Whereas all the men inhabiting the townships of Gweder and Penmaghnow in the Commote of the lord King of Nantconwey in the County of Carnarvon have from the time of which the memory of man is not to the contrary had and used an old custom amongst themselves that none of them should keep more grazing cattle than they were able to keep in the winter, nevertheless (and here took the beasts and cattle of strange and foreign men to the number of one hundred) and these they kept during the time of summer upon a certain common belonging to the township called Molleshabbowe (and Dollolian) . . . to the injury both of the free tenants there and of all other inhabitants in the same townships and contrary to the aforesaid custom.

Court records were often couched in colourful terms, as was this presentment dated May 1630. It gives a lively picture of a woman defendant and the difficulty one of the bailiffs had in apprehending her and bringing her to court:

Item, the said defendant (Kathryn Jeffrey) did cale Alce Price, the wife of William Stodart of Carnarvon, merchant, vidzt dihirog, bydrog and Coegan naughtipake and all the fowle words she could devis . . .

Item, the said defft. Kathryn Jeffrey being apprehended by John Rowland one of the sergiantes att mace in the towne of Carnarvon by the commaund of William Robinson gent one of the bailiffes of the said Towne and Liberties of Carnarvon, refused to goe with the said sergiant he havinge taken her by the Cloake yett could he not stay her.

The damage done by wildlife to the farmer is no new problem. As early as 1649 Justices had to levy a rate in order to finance payment to those who could prove they had killed vermin:

That this Countie beinge a mountainous & Rockie Country havinge in it places not accessible until without greate difficultie wch wth other Coverts is a breedinge place of Grayes Otters Wilde Catts hedgehogges polecattes fitchewes wessells stotes or faire bade ravens and crowes & a receptackle & a place of refuge for them upon any disturbance of them by hunters; by wch means they are & proove to be a greate & unspeakable destrucon of sheeps of all ages, of Geese & all sorts of poultrie of games as of partridges and growces & fish etc to the greate damage & losse of the inhabitants of this County noe place of the County being free from all or any of these sortes of vermines . . . or noysome beasts & wch of late yeeres are growne numerous the greater occasions of moste of the inhabitantes of the Countrey not admittinge them tyme to attende the hunting of them . . .

The Justices levied a rate on the county to pay people to kill the vermin. Returns had to be certified by a minister and the churchwardens of the parishes before payment could be made.

Various crimes and misdemeanours kept the constables busy. The work was demanding, and as it was unpaid we read occasionally of a constable appealing against his appointment and Justices, men of property themselves who often farmed, were sympathetic to many of these appeals which came from yeomen or lesser gentry with similar responsibilities.

Not all the Justices' work dealt with crime. They did have their humanitarian tasks. Before there was talk of a Board of Guardians or a workhouse, they operated the Poor Law. After the dissolution of the monasteries it was their responsibility to offer succour to the poor where needed:

> Jane ych Morgan ordered to be put prentice to Robert Davd ap Nicholas either for vijen (years) or till shee to be married. Richard ap W'm a poore ladd to be put prentice for vijen years to Robt. Jones Joyner.

Prisoners' pleas for help came in many forms. One typical, here quoted, was an attempt to procure a dire necessity:

> Gentlemen . . . I am sorry to say that I have to make abblication for a pair of shoes my shoes was good when I first came heare but during the space of nine weeks which I have been confined they are entirely done and having know to work on the treadmill I am in great pain as they will not stay on my feet and being unable to get a pair myself I therefore appeal to ye as the county magistrates.
>
> Owen Owens, prisoner, March 1835.

Their work in assessing suitability for pension for maimed and wounded soldiers was more difficult, as many would-be recipients considered the Justices to be a soft option and worth an attempt to solicit financial help, even though their so-called war wounds were never received on the battlefield.

After the Restoration in 1661 Caernarfon Justices received an order:

> That Major William Spicer, William Thomas, Aldermen of Carnarvon & William Robins, gentleman, call all the petitioners or maymed soldiers before them & looke who are the most deserving reliefe by their maymes and woundes.

Thirty three cases were examined. Four were given a pension.

Robert Owen was one:

> Robert Owen of Caerhun maymed of the hand and wounded
> on the head in Nasbie fight, a very poor man.

Organising the levying and collection of rates, issuing licences, maintaining the fabric of the Shire Hall and the County Gaol, even tracking down Papists at a certain point in history, as well as dealing with crime in its many forms, made the life of a Justice of the Peace a busy one indeed.

Quarter Sessions in the 16th century

Quarter Sessions records consist of 'presentments', 'indictments' and 'writs'. Those appertaining to Caernarfon may be read in English translation from Latin at the Gwynedd County Record Office.

Presentments were cases first presented to a Justice who then considered whether there was sufficient evidence to warrant a trial. If so, they then became indictments.

Caernarfon at the beginning of the 16th century was a busy market town and port. The variety of cases considered by the courts following the introduction of the new legal system in 1536 mirrored the social scene. For instance, there were always those out to make a quick profit on a market day. Merchants from away would plan to visit the markets of Caernarfonshire with staple goods always in demand, only to be forestalled sometimes before they reached the town by others willing to buy on the road, and then sell at inflated prices themselves at the market.

'John ap David ap Hywel ap Thomas, lately of Nevin in the county aforesaid, gentleman' announced the presentment, 'on the 24th day of May in the 33rd year of the reign of the Lord Henry the Eighth in the grace of God . . . with force and arms etc. at Carnarvon aforesaid in the County aforesaid fore-stalled diverse men being lieges of the Lord the King coming to the market of Carnarvon with six casks of salt and bought that salt before it came to the aforesaid market to the great detriment, harm and injury of the burgesses of the aforesaid town and contrary to the peace and to the statute in respect thereof lately ordained, made and provided.'

Salt was not the only commodity of value. On another occasion:

'Richard ap John ap Wyn, on 29th November in the 33rd year of the reign of the Lord Henry VIII . . . with force and arms at Ceidio, met and forestalled divers lieges of the Lord and King coming to the markets of the towns of Nevin, Pwllheli and Cricieth with untanned leather, wool and corn . . . to the great injury of the burgesses of the aforesaid towns . . . contrary to the peace.' etc. etc.

In the latter case, the indictment had the added endorsement 'fined'.

Quarter Sessions records tell of assaults on bailiffs as they attempted to collect revenues. Bailiffs received little respect from the public.

The bare necessities of life were often stolen, but the thieves received no quarter from the courts, although today their crimes would be considered insignificant – stealing a shirt, a tunic, gloves, woollen clothing, a sheep, as well as small amounts of money. However small they may appear to us today, these items had their value in the economy of the 16th century.

In 1536 Ieuan ap Moris of Castell, labourer, stole a linen sheet worth fourpence. Elin verch Llywelyn ap David, spinster of Penmorfa, was found guilty of stealing a sheep worth ten pence. Elin was sentenced to be whipped around Penmorfa, then released.

Some sentences were particularly cruel. In 1557 Margaret Ieuan ap David Madog was charged and found guilty of stealing a cheese. She was sentenced to spend time in the stocks, then publicly subjected to the excruciating pain of having a nail driven into her ear.

Branding on the hand was another punishment. The sex of the guilty person was not considered. The depth of the burning depended on the severity of the crime. Even branding 'with a cool iron' was horrifying.

During the 16th century the prison cells in the castle were rarely used, except perhaps to hold those accused before trial and those who had to face execution. Sentences usually consisted of fines, periods in the stocks, whippings and floggings.

Misappropriation of cattle was the cause of several cases to be considered by justices and juries. In 1550 it was claimed that:

Thomas ap John ap Gruffydd ap Hywel of Glasfryn, yeoman, at Glasfryn unlawfully broke and entered the stable or pound of John ap Rhys Vaughan and moved out and took away one horse and one foal, the property of the said Thomas, which the said John finding on his land had recently impounded on account of trespass and damages.

Where would the Justice's sympathy lie? With the owner of the horse and foal or the man on whose land they had strayed? We are not told.

Some charges of assault were vividly described. In 1553 a group of men – Robert ap John ap Harri ap Gwilym of Eirianws, labourer, and Rhys ap Harri ap Gwilym, yeoman, assaulted Henry ap Edward ap William of Dwygyfylchi and Thomas ap Robert ap Llywelyn 'with swords, staves, bows and arrows', and 'with a stretched bow then and there shot with an arrow the said Thomas and the arrow struck him on the forehead and broke the scalp of his head and gave him a great wound so that for a long time he languished in danger of death.'

An endorsement to the indictment states that the court found the parties guilty but no mention is made of sentence. Perhaps it was passed to the Assizes for decision, as was often done with severe cases.

In the Quarter Sessions papers for this century is a writ for the jury dated 1554 where the sheriff ordered to come before the Justices of the Peace on the following Wednesday 'twelve free and lawful men from the neighbourhood of Llanfairfechan, to inquire whether William ap Morgan of Llanfairfechan, yeoman, kept cards and dice in his house and permitted various men to play at cards

and dice and at other unlawful games and contrary to the Statute.'
It was stipulated that none of those called was to be a relative of
the accused.

An endorsement to the writ reads 'they say upon their oath that
William Morgan is not guilty in the manner and form alleged and
so he is discharged.'

Vagabonds – and there were many – were considered to be a
plague on society. In 1569 'John Lewis ap Hoell ap Ier, vagabond,
is to be comitted to the Constable of the Peace of the commote of
Issaph, ordered to be brought to the pillory and there stand an
houre and then whipped and sent to his parish.'

Quarter Sessions
in the 17th and 18th centuries

The reigns of Henry VIII and Elizabeth I saw great changes in Britain. It was a cruel time, with many executions of those who were figureheads at Court and in the church. Mary, Queen of Scots was executed, as was Ann Boleyn. Bishops Latimer and Ridley were burned at the stake.

Drake and Raleigh were making a name for themselves at sea. Henry VIII dissolved the monasteries.

The 17th century saw the English Civil Wars. Shakespeare was writing, and died in 1616. Cromwell became Protector. The Great Plague decimated London's population, to be followed by the Great Fire.

Yet how much of this infiltrated over the border to the far-flung country districts of Caernarfonshire? The gentry travelled, and some were involved in events in England, but the life of the common people, the poor, continued its hard, relentless grind, and this was reflected in cases heard in the courts.

Petty Sessions, Quarter Sessions and Assizes in Caernarfon were kept busy. The records bring to light cases which paint a picture of unrest on the land, in commerce, and the hard economic times, with Justices of the Peace needing to be all things to all men. Not all the indictments we can read today are endorsed with the sentences passed, but those which are noted tell a sorry tale.

What was the story behind a charge made by Marghit verch Rees ap Owen upon two men who 'entered the church of

Llanveirvechan and dug up the grave of Edward Price, newly buried'?

The system of payment to those killing vermin in the countryside, mentioned previously, still applied a century later:

Richard Thomas and Richard Price, Llanrhychwyn, petition the court as huntsmen that they keep dogs for the killing and destroying of vermin. Note that they have killed 30 foxes in the comotte of Nantconwy last May and previously killed 22 foxes and cubbs at Dolwythelan, Bettws, Caerhun, Trefriw, Aber and in the township of Gwedyr and complain that they have not been paid any allowance.'

An endorsement stated 'nothing done upon this petition'. Maybe the petitioners had omitted to seek the official confirmation of the various churchwardens necessary before payment could be authorised.

Some of those in need of help to live their lives approached the Bench for assistance. People like Elizabeth Rushen of Conwy, a widow who wrote pleading for money to pay for her and her two children to travel to London 'to see what is due to her after her husband, a soldier, was killed by a corporal.' And a petition from Owen ap Robert ap William of Llanrhychwyn, a farmer who wished to be 'freed from appointment as High Constable of Nant Conway due to the fact that he is very poore and has a wife and four small children to support.'

Robert ap William John of Aberdaron was eager to expand his catering business, and applied for a licence 'to sell in his victualling house where he accommodates horse and foot.'

Cases of misdemeanour and crime were varied. William Jones, 'late of Llananigan', pleaded not guilty to assaulting Henry ap Hugh 'by throwing a cup of drink in his face.' The court did not allow his plea, and fined him two shillings, a sum he would have found difficult to spare if he were a labourer.

The grazing rights for sheep and cattle were often the subject of court disputes, as they had been a century earlier. In 1649 Howell Thomas of Maen y Castell was accused of taking bribes from the tenants of an estate to allow them to graze cattle on his master's land.

Witchcraft was feared. Two indictments concerned Rhydderch ap Evan, Llannor (yeoman); Lowry verch Evan, the wife of Evan Vaughan, Llanbedrog (yeoman); Agnes verch Evan, who appeared before the court in Caernarfon in 1616. The complicated wording of the charge reads:

> On diverse days and times, as well before as after, having not God before their eyes but being reduced by the instigation of the Devil voluntarily and of their malice aforethought, certain wicked and diabolical arts called witchcraft Enchantment Charms and Sorceries wickedly devilishly feloniously and contrary to the laws of God at Llanbedrog aforesaid in the said county did exercise use and practise with an intent to destroy, waste, pine, consume and lame the body of one Mary Hughes late of Llanbedrog aforesaid in the county aforesaid, spinster, by reason whereof the said Mary from the said first day of August in the year aforesaid did from that time, continually hitherto in her body did consume waste and pine and became lame in her left arm and both her feet and wholly and altogether lost the use of her tongue and voice, to the grievous damage of the said Mary and against the Peace of our said Lord the King his Crown and Dignities, and also against the form of the Statute in such case made and provided.'

A second indictment reads:

> 'On the 20th day of June in the 19th year of the Reign of our Sovereign Lord James and on diverse other days and times', using witchcraft as before, these persons did 'use and practise with an intent to slay and kill one Margaret Hughes late of Llanbedrog aforesaid in the said county, spinster, reasons of which the said Margaret from the said 20th day of June in the year aforesaid to the first day of January then next following at Llanbedrog aforesaid in the said county did languish, on which first day of January in the said year the aforesaid Margaret by

24

reason of the practising and exercising the wicked and diabolical Arts aforesaid at Llanbedrog aforesaid in the said County, died.'

The verdict was 'Guilty', and the sentence curt and to the point . . . 'suspendatur' (to be hanged). Their execution at Pont Seiont would have been an event of much rejoicing, as the fear of witchcraft was so great.

The sentence passed on hapless Maurice Humphrey of Llangian in 1690 was signed by four Justices. The Clerk of the Peace went into great detail:

Whereas Maurice Humphrey late of Llangian was this day by his owne confession convicted at this General Sessions of the Peace for wilfully besteing and assaulting his master Hugh Hughes gent. contrary to the forme of the statute in yt case made . . . it is ordered by this Court that the said Maurice Humphrey be upon Saturday the 19th day of this instant July conveyed to the Crosse lieing in the market town of Pwllhely in this County and then and there between the houres of ten of the clock in the morning and two in the afternoone of the same day be stript naked from the waist upward and tied to a carr drawne with a horse and soe striped and tied publickly drawne along the High Street and whipt from the said Crosse as far as the house of Richard Arthur in the said towne of Pullhely till his body be bloody and that a warrant be issued forth with the Sheriff of this County to put this order in execution.

A declamation of 1655 tells the story of abduction and clandestine marriage, sufficient to be a plot for a 19th century novel!

John Jones of Trevan was unlawfully married to Elizabeth Annwyl Jane Wynne of Llanverch y Gest, widow, the former being an orphan and a minor. The marriage was performed by a minister and then by Edmund Glynne JP without due publication or registration. Declared on information of

Gruffydd Jones, gent., register of the church of Crickieth and on confession of Elizabeth Annwyl that she and Ellis Roberts of Nysken, gent, did by fraud steale and take away John Jones with intent to marry him . . . with judgment that the marriage be null and void that Elizabeth Annwyl and Ellis Roberts forfeit half their estate to the Commonwealth and half to John Jones and that they be imprisoned.

There is no mention of the minister being charged, unlike the following:

William Jones of Aberpwll, clerk in holy order, was arrested as he hath committed and made diverse clandestine marriages and married diverse mens childrens and servantes in ale houses and other unfitting places without banes asked or licences had from thordinary and without consent of parents to the great damadge and discomfort of diverse of his mates subjects of the evil example of others in like manner offending.

Some charged with a crime were imprisoned in Caernarfon to await their trial. Others were bailed on surety until the case could be heard. One petition was made to the magistrates on behalf of Ellis Jones and William James of Caernarfon who had agreed to be sureties for John Bright, late of Caernarfon, who was to appear at the Quarter Sessions, but in the meantime he had absconded to Ireland, so was unlikely to appear. In normal circumstances often substantial sums would have to be paid. But in this case a petition went to the Sessions stating 'The sympathy of the Justices is requested for Evan Jones and William James who are butt poore men'.

Assaults, affrays, the upkeep of bastard children, theft, and vagrancy all continued to concern the Justices at courts in the 18th century.

There were cases which appear to us to have been a waste of Justices' time, but in those days were deemed important.

In 1700 John Owen and John Roberts prosecuted Richard Griffith 'for speaking scandalous words of the said J. Owens . . .

and charging him with hearkening under the window of Ellin Meredith alias Evans widdow, on Wednesday being the 11th of September in the night time.'

Three men were charged with causing 'a bloody affray on the Lords day, being the Wake day at Llaniestyn.'

It was not only men who were charged with assault or affray. In 1748 High and Petty constables and other officers of the Peace in the county were ordered to apprehend Margaret Nicholas of Caernarfon, spinster, and bind her over to appear at the next Quarter Sessions to answer 'for beating Prudence, the wife of John Jones of Carnarvon, mariner, and to imprison her if she refuses.'

A petition from Robert Foulk of Llandwrog, yeoman, was heard 'for relief towards the maintenance of the base child of Maurice Wynne of Bryn yr Odin, pa. Llandwrog, gent, which he has maintained and kept for the previous eight years. The said Maurice Wynne not having paid the yearly sum of forty shillings promised for that purpose.'

Margaret, the wife of Thomas Prichard Meredith of Bryncroes, labourer, was charged with stealing wool worth ten pence from John Owen, another labourer. He later accused her of stealing 1½lbs wool from his barn and she was to be imprisoned until her trial, but she was discharged before the Sessions as there was not sufficient evidence against her.

The county's bridges needed repair, as in 1701 when the Sessions were informed by 'John Evans and David Thomas both of Llanbeder that the bridges called Pont y Camma and Pontrhyd y bedde, both situated on the road between Coneway and Llanrwst, are in need of repair.'

Vagrants continued to be a thorn in the flesh of local authorities. There are several notices and orders to constables, paying them to convey vagrants to Beaumaris on their way to Ireland. It was, presumably, cheaper to do this than to allow them to stay and be a drain on the parishes.

Although relatively unimportant cases were heard at the Quarter Sessions, some were passed over to Assizes for judgment – there were some two hundred offences which could result in a death sentence. Escape from prison was one, especially if the prisoner was awaiting transportation overseas and was determined to avoid it at all costs. John, the husband, of Margery, a tinker from Ro-wen was one. He was caught in Denbighshire, brought back to Caernarfon Gaol, tried for escaping and duly sentenced. He is said to have sung verses of his own composition about his capture as he mounted the scaffold.

Two men were executed for mutiny in 1758, and a year later a character known as 'Civil Wil' received a similar sentence for robbing a shop in Beddgelert.

Harsh sentences such as these continued until the 19th century, when reform took place.

The 19th and early 20th centuries

The 19th and early 20th centuries saw wars, an industrial revolution and great changes in society, yet life in the remote country districts of Caernarfonshire went on largely unaffected. Caernarfon developed as a port, thanks to the burgeoning slate industry in the Nantlle valley, its quayside busy as slates were unloaded from the railway to be transferred to the holds of coastal vessels which had previously been emptied of everyday necessities. Access across country was still difficult. It was easier to convey goods by sea.

There was poverty still, reflected in the cases of petty theft which appeared before Caernarfon magistrates. More often than not those found guilty were formally fined with the option of having to undergo a short prison sentence if they could not afford to pay. Although prison sentences were short, if accompanied by hard labour they could be severe. It was not until later in the 19th century that sentences for petty crimes were reviewed, so convictions remained harsh until then.

Transportation to the colonies for more serious crimes was feared. This continued until 1853 when some of the colonies found themselves over-manned with convicts and refused to take more, so it was no longer possible to use this 'out of sight, out of mind' policy. Yet, while it was still operated, it did not dissuade some criminals. John Lloyd of Llanbeblig stole a watch, five pairs of woollen stockings, two silk handkerchiefs, one cotton handkerchief, a shirt and a pair of drawers, a knife and a razor from Owen Pierce, a mariner, and was transported for seven years, the usual length of time. Working as a labourer in a strange country so far overseas, it was unlikely that he would save enough money to pay his passage back home at the end of the sentence.

In 1831 Richard Parry was transported for stealing a silver watch, yet at the same sessions David Jones, a labourer, was sentenced to two months imprisonment with hard labour for stealing a watch and a pair of shoes and 'to be whipped privately at the expiration of his sentence'. Why a different sentence for what would appear to be a similar crime?

Women frequently appeared in court, usually charged with theft. Anne Jones had to spend six weeks in prison with hard labour in 1869 for stealing a metal teapot, while another Ann, Ann Hughes, was sentenced to one month in gaol for the theft of three loaves of bread. Times were hard.

Clothes and fabrics provided a temptation to some women. Elizabeth Roberts, a widow, spent three months in Caernarfon Gaol for stealing a woollen shawl and a piece of cloth. Ellin Owen received a similar sentence for the theft of ten yards of velveteen and ten yards of linsey from a shop.

Women were sometimes brought before the Bench to answer to a charge of assault. Elizabeth Williams, the wife of a quarryman of Llanddeiniolen, was one. She was accused and found guilty of assaulting and beating Elizabeth Jones of Brynrefail. She was ordered to pay for the offence and the costs of the trial to Elizabeth Jones.

Women of easy virtue were not tolerated in Victorian society. Catherine Roberts spent twenty-one days in gaol with hard labour, for 'being an indecent person and a common prostitute'.

There were many cases of sheep stealing, those found guilty usually being given prison sentences of up to eighteen months.

Drunkenness was rife. The House of Correction at Caernarfon Gaol dealt with these culprits by keeping them behind bars for short periods, returning them to society duly sobered, but for how long?

Caernarfon court heard many bastardy cases, where the father was ordered to pay maintenance. Desertion of the family was another situation handled by the magistrates. Robert Williams, in

1831, received a sentence of one month in prison with hard labour, and was ordered to pay Pwllheli Poor Law Union £1.6s.3d – could this have been the cost of maintenance for one month?

Vagrants and beggars could always be found in Caernarfon Gaol. William Kelly spent seven days in the House of Correction, with hard labour, for being 'an idle person' and unlawfully soliciting alms. Many were imprisoned for up to six weeks. Mahomey Swales was convicted for vagrancy and 'deceiving the public with palmistry'. David Davies, a Bangor labourer, had been a vagrant but found refuge in the Bangor & Beaumaris Union Workhouse, from where he stole moleskin trousers and a moleskin jacket valued at five shillings, belonging to the Guardians of the Poor of the Union. His sentence was six weeks in prison.

A strange sentence in 1851 concerned two labourers of Llannor who were found guilty of stealing 15lbs of barley valued at 9d. They had to spend a month in prison with hard labour, and to be 'well whipped and to be kept separate from the other felons in the gaol'.

During a random search through Quarter Sessions records for the century the only case noted of a child in court was recorded in 1850 when John Paylheich, aged 10, was found guilty of the theft of one shilling and five sixpences, for which he was to be in gaol for eight hours 'and to be whipped once privately'.

Not all those charged were convicted. When the Britannia Bridge was being built two men were charged with stealing ten pounds of iron from the Chester and Holyhead Railway Company, but there was insufficient evidence so the case was dismissed.

Even before the days of the motor car, there were road offences. Jane Jones of Bangor was fined for allowing her donkey to stray on to the high road. John McKivett of Edeyrn was fined five shillings with ten shillings costs, or, if he was unable to pay, to be kept in gaol for seven days for 'driving an omnibus furiously and endangering lives' (a horse-driven omnibus, of course). There were also convictions for ill-treating horses.

There is record of a conviction for driving a cart on the highway without anyone on foot to guide the horse, and another for using a cart without the owner's name painted on the outside.

The county's long coastline saw many wrecks in the days of sail. In the 19th century wrecks had to be reported to the authorities, but local people still helped themselves to whatever, still usable, wreckage was washed ashore after a storm, as they had done for centuries although by this time that, too, was illegal.

Griffith Owen Roberts was reported for not informing the Receiver of Wrecks when he came across a beam and planks at Pwllheli. He was sentenced to two weeks' imprisonment. Another man was found guilty of 'carrying away' the wreckage from a ship and sent to gaol for one month.

Before 1869, when county councils came into being, the magistrates had other responsibilities as well as sitting on the Bench to hear criminal cases. They had to grant licences – John Robson was granted a licence 'to open a theatre in Bangor performing for a number of days not exceeding sixty'.

Inn and public house licences were issued. The magistrates had to sanction payment for public works such as road and bridge repairs, fuel for use at Caernarfon Barracks, and paying the town crier.

In 1818 there is a record of the court's dealings with the Coroner's inquisitions for the year – regarding Hugh Jones of Llandygái who died in a slate quarry accident; John Evans of Betws Garmon who was found dead in a barn; Owen Jones of Llandwrog who died in his sleep; an unknown man whose body was washed ashore at Pistyll; Richard Roberts, an infant of Llangian, who died attempting to ford the river Soch; John Roberts of Llangian who poisoned himself inadvertently by taking arsenic to cure a headache, and Evan Lloyd of Betws Garmon who suffered a fractured skull and died after he fell from scaffolding.

Time passed. A new century dawned. But human frailty continued to cause theft, assault, and a continuance of many of the charges made against defendants appearing at the Caernarfon courts in previous centuries.

One case brings the story of the magistrates almost up to the date Caernarfon Gaol closed in 1921. This happened at the start of the first world war in 1914, when William John Jones falsely informed Anne Parry that he was on sick leave from the army and

Inner prison tower in the colonial days of Caernarfon castle

The old door to the prison tower – this is now the location of the castle shop

The ruins of Caernarfon castle today, showing its strategic position on the shore of the Menai Strait

The old police headquarters (left) and Caernarfon Crown Court from the castle walls

The Court entrance

The Scales of Justice on the ridge

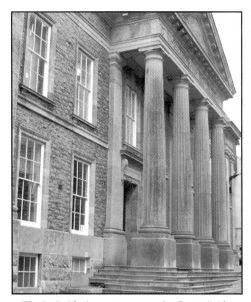

The intimidating entrance to the Court in the old Shire Hall

The entrance to the old Police HQ

The neo-classical style belonged to the Victorian era

Caernarfonshire Police, inspected within the castle walls, 1929

A group of Caernarfonshire police in front of the old gaol

Group of policemen in Caernarfon castle with Superintendent/Deputy Chief Constable Samuel Thomas Harris (1855-1936) c. 1890

A group of Caernarfonshire police in the castle c. 1890

Staff of Caernarfon Gaol in the Gaol grounds. Ann Pritchard, head wardress sits on the extreme left in the front row – she administered to the last female prisoner to be hanged in Caernarfon. 1890s.

Staff of Caernarfon Gaol with Ann Pritchard seated on the right, just before the Gaol closed. c. 1922

CARNARVON NEW GAOL.

CONTRACT Nọ 2.

Parties desirous of Tendering for the Works comprised in Contract No. 2 of the above works, which includes the taking down of a portion of the Old Gaol, and Erecting and Completing the North East Wing of the New Gaol, are requested to send in Sealed Tenders to the Clerk of the Peace on or before Wednesday the 16th day of October, 1867, specifying the amount of their Tender, and the names and addresses of two responsible parties as Sureties, who will be required to enter into a Bond in one fourth of the Sum Contracted for, to complete the work and perform the Contract, according to the Plans, Specifications and Conditions, which may be inspected at the Offices of Mr. John Thomas, County Surveyor, No. 11 Market Street, Carnarvon.

The Lowest Tender will not necessarily be accepted.

Carnarvon, 16th September, 1867.

WILLIAM THEARSBY POOLE,

Clerk of the Peace.

·PRINTED AT THE CHIEF CONSTABLE'S OFFICE, CARNARVON.

A poster inviting tenders for building works in Caernarfon Gaol, issued by the Clerk of the Peace. 16 September, 1867

The harbour, Trefor, with a steamer being loaded with sets and the sailing ship Jane & Ann *waiting to load. In 'Doc Bach' can be seen one of the sailing ships which used to carry stones to the goal at Caernarfon for the prisoners to grind.*

The gallows' tower on the Menai side of the town walls

William Murphy, the last man to be hanged in Caernarfon Gaol, 1910

The old gallows' tower today

The old Gaol door still seen
in Stryd y Jêl, Caernarfon

The old Caernarfon Gaol now houses county offices

The present Crown Court at Caernarfon

May 16. 1857 — At Gaol. Present Llewn
Rowlands Eq. & Revd W. Williams —

Walmsley Sworn. —

Smith said to me "give me my jacket." I
said it was against orders." He said "I should
like to punch your head for you " — ——
—— After further altercation he said
"Go home ofuick you bloody German Wretch
"or else tell Bigon to do it & get some
new Wretches" — Upon inspecting his
Cell I find he had broken the bread box
off from the Wall — also that he took
up some part of the Stone Flagging from in
floor of the Cell & broke it. ——

Walker sworn — I put Smith in his Cell
for solitary confinement — I observed the
State of the Floor as usual — Afterwards
I observed that part of the Flags were loose
I also observed the Bed was in its usual
State — It's now broken —

Walmsley. cont.d — He told me he would
break his Bench — & next day I found it was
broken. —

Memorandum regarding threats made by a prisoner, George Smith, to a 'turnkey' or Gaoler called Walmsley Smith, is alleged to have used disgusting language and to having broken his 'bed, bench and wall'. Walmsley's statement (taken by the Rev. W. Williams and Rowlands Esq.) with regard to the incident.

Penyberth in Llŷn, the old mansion house destroyed by the Ministry of Defence to create a Bombing School in 1936.

The memorial at Penyberth today to remember the arson attack of three distinguished Welsh leaders of the period on the Bombing School, which led to a Crown Court prosecution at Caernarfon. The trial was moved to the Old Bailey in London when the jury at Caernarfon refused to find the 'Penyberth Three' guilty.

*D.J. Williams, Lewis Valentine and Saunders Lewis
spent a year at Wormwood Scrubs' prison in London,
following their action at Penyberth.*

*The grand welcoming party at the Pavilion, Caernarfon for the 'Penyberth Three',
on their release from prison in September 1937.*

The 1980s arson attacks on holiday homes were the background to another famous trial at Caernarfon: the case of the 'Gwynedd Three', when members of MI6 were forced to give evidence at a trial for the first time.

Dewi Prysor – freed after being detained for 15 months

'Stwmp' – also found not guilty at the trial

Siôn Aubrey – imprisoned for 12 years

required board and lodging for which the government would pay. The court decided that the crime was committed with intent to defraud Anne Parry of £1.3s.0d and Jones was sent to Caernarfon Gaol for three months with hard labour.

Persistent offenders

During the mid- and late-19th century Caernarfon was a town with two faces – the prosperous Victorians inhabiting grand new villas on the town's fringes, and those to whom dire poverty was a fact of life. Caernarfon had its seamy side, as did any port, large or small. Very many of the cases appearing before the Justices reflected this. Serious crime was relatively rare, but the court saw many petty thefts and cases of drunkenness which received fines or short periods of imprisonment.

Certain characters frequented the courtroom over and over again. Reading the presentments to Quarter Sessions and the newspaper reports of court proceedings it seems as though the Justices were sometimes at their wits' end to impress the persistent offenders with the folly of their lifestyle, as often as not to no avail.

Robert Roberts, known in the town as Bob Robin, was one of those who appeared before the Bench with predictable regularity. The *Caernarfon & Denbigh Herald* gave column inches to reporting his misdemeanours and the exhortations of the Justices when passing sentence. Brawls were frequent, and Bob Robin could often be found in the centre of the action.

In the early 1840s the newspaper reported:

PUNISHMENT IN THE STOCKS . . . The punishment of confining persons in the stocks, which had been done away with for some time, was last Friday inflicted on a well-known character of the town, called Bob Robin, from ten o'clock till three in the afternoon, for having refused to pay a fine which had been inflicted on him for drunkenness. We predict that though he has been reeling since he has been freed, he will presently be steadied by another dose of the same wholesome corrective.

The reporter knew his subject. A few days after his release from the stocks Bob Robin was charged with drunkenness once again.

In May 1860 Bob Robin's name appeared again in the Sessions list, this time for assaulting a policeman when that officer was trying to make an arrest. For this he was sentenced for the 53rd time, Justice Llewelyn Turner remarking:

As to you Robert Roberts your career is an extra ordinary one, it is a melancholy picture of the depth of degradation to which a man may bring himself. You have lived the life of a vagabond on the face of the earth. You were discharged from the common gaol at 11 o'clock yesterday, after being incarcerated within its walls fifty two times, half of your manhood has been spent there, and it would be well for you, well for the legion of persons whom you have injured and annoyed had the whole instead of half your time passed under restraint. I wish that anything I would say, any sentence this court could pass, might tend to reform you, for it is dreadful to conceive what must be the end of such a person.

August of the same year saw Bob Robin in court again, on a charge of being 'drunk and riotous'. Llewelyn Turner's comments on passing the three month's sentence were:

Robert Roberts, I deeply regret to see you here again. You have, it seems, this time been one week out of gaol, during a portion of which you succeeded in annoying a great number of people and creating an amount of disturbance, which cannot be allowed in the streets of any town. It is said, and it must be evident, that you are not in a position to purchase drink, and I have received reliable information that it is given to you by others. It is disgraceful in the extreme to those who so act, to those who selfishly injure your body and soul, by giving you drink for the sake of beholding your folly . . . I say it advisedly, they are responsible for the acts you commit, and you may in measure thank them for the punishment you are about to undergo. It seems that during your later bouts of drunkenness you have suffered from very severe fits. Reflect when sober upon the horror of being cut off in such a state. You must pay a fine of forty shillings or in default go to gaol for three months.

Here, the prisoner asked for a fortnight to pay, to which the Justice responded:

In justice to yourself not a day, restraint is the only hope. Again I say, you may thank those that gave you drink for your continued imprisonment. I wish the law could reach them, I can do no more than ask the reporters at the table to give publicity to my expressions with regard to them.

The newspapers kept the Bob Robin stories running for some years. In 1872 he offended again, this time receiving a sentence of a month in prison for being drunk and disorderly and for absconding from the workhouse. What was his end? That we do not know.

Transportation cut short what could well have been another persistent offender's nefarious activities. She was Margaret Presdee who first appeared in court in 1840, charged with and convicted of stealing a man's purse while he was drinking in one of the town's public houses. Four years later came another conviction, this time for assault, and she was then fined ten shillings with ten shillings costs, but because she could not pay, spent a month in Caernarfon Gaol. Her third and final conviction was when she was found guilty of receiving stolen goods from a drapery shop in the town. All three convictions were taken into account when the Bench passed judgment, and she was sent to Tasmania for seven years.

The apprentice in the shop, who had taken the goods on her behalf, was sentenced to six months in gaol with hard labour. The

Caernarfon & Denbigh Herald reporter must have relished the Justice's comment:

'It is hoped that the disgraceful and most onerous position in which this youth is now placed will tend in others to check that indiscretion (to use the mildest term) which not only sloped to him the path of crime, but impelled him down its ruinous declivity. Amongst the many modes of extravagance, folly, and sin that lead to crime,' he continued, referring to Margaret Presdee, 'the sacred moralist has assured us that the company of the lewd woman is the most dangerous, and fearful – ruin, death and judgment are the results of her endearments, and her smile is a yawning sepulchre, engulphing every virtue and every hope.'

Margaret Presdee was one of sixteen women transported to the other side of the world from Caernarfon.

Caernarfon's prisons

In the days before Henry VIII's new justice system came into being, miscreants were kept in the castle to await trial. Sentences in those early days were usually fines, whippings, a period in the stocks, pillory or ducking stool. Incarceration for long periods was unusual.

As the magisterial system became the norm a purpose-built gaol was erected close to the town wall. This was the prison building criticised so sharply by reformer John Howard, who visited every prison in the country. He arrived in Caernarfon in 1782, and had this to say in his report to Parliament:

> This gaol, which is also the Bridewell, was formerly a chapel and is in a ruinous condition. Two rooms for debtors and two for felons; one of the latter down 11 steps with an aperture 18 inches by 31, the other under the stairs only 9 feet by 7, with no window, all of them very dirty, and never white-washed. Joining to the gaol is a large room, formerly a house of correction, but lately used by strolling players. A court but no sewer, no water. Neither clauses against spiritous liquors, nor the act for preserving the health of prisoners, are hung up. The gaoler has £5 a year as keeper of Bridewell. He stops from each felon's allowance sixpence a week, what he calls his 'trouble of weekly payment'. No table of fees.

In those days prisoners were at the mercy of the gaoler who could regulate the amount of food they received. It paid to be in his favour, so a weekly donation helped to this end. The gaoler's dominance in prison life came to an end when Howard's reforms were introduced.

John Howard concluded:

Among the various improvements that are making in this town may it not be hoped that the county magistrates will think of a better prison.

His report must have tweaked the conscience of the authorities in Caernarfon, as before long an advertisement appeared in the *Chester Chronicle* inviting tenders for 'the rebuilding of Carnarvon Gaol. Subject to such conditions shall be then agreed upon. A plan of the said Gaol may be seen and further particulars had at the Clerk of the Court's office in Carnarvon.'

The contract went to a Mr Pierce of Wrexham, and work began immediately. The new prison was ready for occupation in 1784.

Rather than praising and being proud of their new gaol, some of the more vociferous townspeople of Caernarfon were critical. They said the prison was too large for requirements. But eventually it had to be rebuilt because it was not large enough. In 1804 a writer described it as 'a neat edifice, looking more like an almshouse'.

When the new Shire Hall was built during the middle of the 19th century the prison was incorporated at the back. It remained in use until 1921 when the building was converted into county offices. One or two of the old cells still remain in the present Crown Court building, to be used on special occasions when felons have to be kept under supervision before trial.

After John Howard's sweeping reforms regular reports on the condition of gaols and their administration had to be made to Parliament. The report for 1833 regarding Caernarfon Gaol makes interesting reading.

Cholera had broken out in the prison during the previous year, when there were seven cases, of which two inmates died and five recovered. One man suffered from typhus fever but after a serious illness lasting six weeks he recovered.

'The general state and regulations of the prison appear to be consistent with the comfort and discipline of the prisoners, as far as the imperfect construction of the Gaol will allow,' commented the inspector.

The gaol was under the direction of the Sheriff, who appointed the Governor, but the magistrates were responsible for the House of Correction where debtors and those guilty of small misdemeanours such as drunkenness were held.

On average Caernarfon Gaol had held 70 prisoners during the previous year, of which there were 17 felons (those charged with having committed serious crimes). The rest were held for lesser crimes and there was a small number of debtors. The greatest number of inmates at one time, it was said, was twenty-four.

One warder was in charge, appointed by the Sheriff to the Common Gaol and by the magistrates to the House of Correction, and a Matron was appointed by the magistrates. A weekly dietary allowance was made to the inmates – two shillings and four pence to criminals and two shillings to debtors. An allowance was also made for clothing and bedding but this 'was uncertain' in 1833. There was no regular employment, but hard labour on the treadmill for five or six hours a day was common, a gruelling punishment. It is not stipulated what part the treadmill played in the life of the prison, apart from punishment. In other prisons, Beaumaris for one, the action of working the mill pumped water into the prison water tanks.

The chaplain had performed divine service twice a week, when prisoners attending – attendance was compulsory – were issued with bibles and Testaments.

The tasks performed without pay, when opportunity arose or need was paramount, included mending clothing, fetching and carrying where necessary, washing and cleaning the building.

Attempts to escape from prison in 1832 had been met by solitary confinement, whipping or placing in irons, but no figures were quoted in the report.

In 1904 Caernarfon prison was visited by R. G. Alford, a civil engineer, who registered his findings in *Notes on the Buildings of English Prisons* (Wales being included). Even through the dry, factual description of the features of the building one can appreciate the atmosphere pervading this dreary place.

When Alford visited, the prison held a daily average of thirty men and thirteen women, and was the second smallest prison in England and Wales. 'It is much congested', he wrote. This building, he reminded the reader, was erected in 1864 under the direction of Sir Llewelyn Turner, 'a county magnate'.

It is situated in Shire Hall Street near the old Castle, with back to the Menai Straits . . . The main building is T-shaped . . . there are three Warders' quarters facing the street . . . The Governor occupies a private house, leased by the Prison Commissioners.

Then follows a detailed description of the building and its yards, the stone used, measurements of the cells, how the prison was heated and lit, and even the colour of the paintwork (particolours for cell doors, pitch-pine varnished for office doors). The cell doors had 'Smith's spring locks with bevelled bolt and two throws, and inspection traps and spys. Mechanical call bells are provided, and the old hammock hooks still remain.' By this time iron bedsteads and mattresses had taken the place of hammocks.

Toilet facilities were poor. 'Two in an annexe, which are the only inside w.cs for male prisoners and there is a sink in the passage which leads to them. This arrangement of prison w.cs in external corners of a basement is "sweet", but inconvenient.'

A double cell was used for manufacturing stores but available on demand as a condemned cell. 'It has two deep windows. A large padded cell is next to the store.'

As in every prison there was a reception area with baths close by as on arrival every prisoner had to strip and bathe, his clothes being stored after fumigation, to be returned to him on release.

After pages of factual description the author strikes a more appreciative note as he writes of the prison chapel:

Over the office passage of the front wing is the interesting little Chapel. It has been nicely decorated with pictures, under the

Chaplain's supervision (the Rev. J. Wynne Jones, vicar of Carnarvon) and has an open stained roof, and skylight. There are open seats with backs, but no kneelers. The women sit on the north side behind a slanting partition, and the floor slopes up westwards. On the east are two windows above the altar, overlooking the roofs, and on the south side is a neat little vestry or Chaplain's office, with a window over the south yards.

The kitchen and laundry are described in detail. In a separate building at ground level was a forge and a carpenter's shop, then:

In the centre of these is the Execution Pit, with high beam over but no bracket, and there is a sheeted iron cover to the pit standing 3½″ above the cement floor. The tower is covered by a centre valley roof.

Prison governors had to report annually to the Secretary of State on the quality of administration. The governor of Caernarfon Gaol in 1910-11 brought the story almost up to the end, as the prison closed in 1921 when there were closures of smaller prisons nationwide.

By 1910-11 administration was more businesslike. The Governor claimed:

The state and discipline of the prison have been satisfactory. The conduct of the prisoners has been good, there being but few reports. No prisoners have been received as offenders of the First Division and only three males and one female as offenders of the Second Division. No juveniles have been received under 16 years of age, but 18 males and 2 females were received between the ages of 16 and 21 years, all with sentences under one month. They have had special attention from the chaplain and myself but sentences being so short only a little improvement could be made.

The power to earn remission is much appreciated, and no doubt encourages good conduct. The system of part payment of fine is still taken advantage of, 21 males having paid. Work in association has been carried out and is very much appreciated.

Male prisoners have been employed at stone-breaking, coal sack-making, mailbag-making, oakum-picking and wood chopping. Female prisoners are employed at washing and repairing clothing, also knitting socks and making shirts. A Mission was held by Captain Spencer of the Church Army. The Discharged Prisoners Aid Society continues its good work. The lady visitor pays special attention to females.

Over a number of years the average number of inmates at Caernarfon remained similar.
The medical officer's report for 1912-13 stated:

The general health of the prisoners has been good. One prisoner, sentenced to 15 months hard labour, has been in the Infirmary since his conviction but his condition is now improving. The equipment of the prison as to ventilation, heating, water supply and clothing has been efficient. The dietary has been of good quality. All the prisoners are examined on admission and discharge.

The health of the prisoners has been exceptionally good. One prisoner was discharged in order to undergo surgical operation for an injury sustained before admission. One prisoner attempted suicide on three occasions.

That year one cell in the male ward and one in the female ward had been adapted for cases of tuberculosis, should they be needed, but no details of how this was done were recorded.
Chaplains took services, were responsible for the restricted amount of education they could dispense as most inmates had short periods of imprisonment. They also assured the Secretary of State, in every report, that lady visitors performed their task more than adequately.

When Caernarfon Gaol closed in 1921 the inmates were transferred elsewhere. After closure the building then became police headquarters for a time and was later adapted as council offices.

Prison rules

Prison rules, laid down for every prison in the country, filled many pages. As well as general rules covering everyday communal life under lock and key, discipline, diet, employment and the responsibilities of visiting justices, there were rules for the Governor, staff, the Matron, Chaplain and Surgeon. Nothing appears to have been left to chance.

Reading these regulations gives a vivid picture of life in gaol, where different categories of inmates were kept separate, as were the sexes. There was no provision for spare time activity – there was no spare time, as prisoners were kept busy at various necessary tasks about the gaol, attending chapel, preparing food, white-washing and cleaning cells and passages, undergoing hard labour.

Those guilty of prison offences, insubordination or refusing to carry out specific work, found themselves punished by being held in dark refactory cells on bread and water, but for no longer than three days at a time. Anyone repeating insubordination could be clapped in irons, but the rules stipulated that this should only be a last resort and a time limit was set.

There were many rules for the visiting Justices to heed. They had to consider appeals from prisoners for certain concessions, and also appeals for mercy before these were passed on for Royal approval or refusal.

The Governor, although in charge of the gaol, was subject to the orders of the visiting Justices. Following the general rule that no alcohol or tobacco was allowed on the premises, the Governor was instructed to be especially wary when friends of prisoners attempted to by-pass the regulation by lowering gifts over the prison wall. He had to be ready to confiscate them. Letters, too, came into this category, as all correspondence delivered in the usual way was opened and read in case it contained anything likely to lead to an escape attempt.

Rule 47 left the Governor in no doubt about what his attitude to the job should be:

He ought to exercise his authority with firmness, temper and humanity, abstain from all irritating language and not strike a prisoner. He must enforce similar conduct on the subordinate officers.

As it happened, events at Caernarfon, as will be seen later, proved that this rule was not always upheld.

The Chaplain had to be a clergyman of the Church of England and all chapel services followed the church calendar. Prisoners of another faith were allowed occasional visits from an appropriate minister. Jews were not expected to work on their Sabbath day.

There were twenty-seven rules for the Surgeon's attention, covering everything from prescribing medication when needed to accompanying the Governor to be present when a prisoner was whipped or underwent any form of corporal punishment.

Rules regarding the behaviour of prisoners were supposed to be printed and hung in a suitable place for all to read, but prison reports over a number of years suggest that this was not always done in Caernarfon.

Governors in trouble

In spite of the rules applying to prison governors, Caernarfon Gaol had two whose standards left much to be desired.

The first complaint came to light in 1843, through a printed statement addressed to Caernarfon magistrates, but eventually distributed more widely in the town. It was written by W. S. Byron of Caernarfon who had been held in the gaol as a debtor for nine months. He accused the Governor, William Henry George, of misconduct on several counts. His statement read:

I charge Mr William Henry George, governor of Carnarvon gaol, with usurping an authority that does not exist even in the magistrates themselves; and with exercising that authority in the most tyrannical and unwarranted manner – to the injustice of the prisoners – to the subversion of order and in total defiance of the prison rules.

I charge him with having practised a deception on the gentlemen of the county, by sending them a different copy of the prison rules from that which is placed in the debtors' wards – there being two distinct copies printed, to the great disadvantage of the debtors, ten are regularly broken with impunity.

I charge him with treating me, in many instances, worse than a criminal, by searching my pockets on entering the prison; causing me to lie on the bare floor at night without a single covering; compelling me to work 11 hours a day, at the same disgraceful employment as felons sentenced to hard labour, and which work has lately been introduced as a substitute for the treadmill; locking me up more than once in solitary confinement, and at one time for five successive days, because I complained to the magistrates; maliciously deceiving me, by telling a most deliberate falsehood respecting the decision of my case by the Society at London; endeavouring to detain me in prison four months longer than my time . . . refusing admission to my friends, and even refusing to let the common necessaries of life be brought to me; and to such an extent did he carry this kind of severity, that had it not been for the support I privately received from my fellow-prisoners I should actually have been starved to death.

I charge him with repeatedly violating the diet regulations, and serving the prisoners with putrified herrings for dinner, which have been thrown into the pig-tub by his own orders – with an unfair distribution of the fund for the relief of discharged criminals – with making criminals work before their trial, and on a Sunday too – with punishing them without cause, and especially if they should happen to complain to the magistrates – with presenting a pistol to one of them in his bed, threatening to blow out his brains – and with refusing to pay debtors, who have for months worked at their own trade.

I charge him with an act of the grossest profanity; namely cutting out, and destroying the leaves of a Bible, because he, more than once, detected the poor criminals endeavouring to derive some consolation from these.

I charge him with the grossest immoralities in his private and public capacity, both in and out of gaol – with habitual drunkenness, and with a misappropriation of the county property and county funds.

I also charge him, in the name of Captain John Owen, of Bangor, with having treated him in the most abusive manner, by placing him in solitary confinement in a room appropriated for the use of felons – and by other acts, equally cruel and unwarranted by the rules.

Byron also accused the visiting magistrates of 'neglect of duty, inattention to enforcement of prison rules, and with gross partiality to the gaoler'.

Prison rules clearly laid down that debtors, not regarded as criminals, were to be treated more leniently than felons. They were housed in a separate ward, called a House of Correction, could wear their own clothes, should not be put to employment as punishment as were the felons, and were entitled to receive gifts of food and comfort from relatives and friends. Apparently Governor George had purposely disregarded these rules. Debtors' stay in prison depended upon how long it took them to discharge their debts.

William Henry George had come to Caernarfon as Governor of the Gaol after a period of service with the Liverpool police force.

Byron's charges were read, with much concern, in Whitehall by the then Secretary of State. An inspector of prisons, the Rev. Whitworth Russell, was despatched to Caernarfon post haste to investigate the complaints, and make his report. The investigation was thorough, taking several days. Twenty-two witnesses were called. As some of these were monoglot Welsh speakers, their testimony had to be translated into English for the benefit of the inspector, which, no doubt, delayed the proceedings.

At the end of the investigation the inspector submitted a lengthy report, concluding:

I am of the opinion that Mr George is not of strictly sober habits; that he has treated with cruelty some of the prisoners committed to his charge; that he has exercised his authority in a vexatious and unlawful manner; that he has permitted, if not promoted, great irregularities in the prison; and venture to submit, for the consideration of the Secretary of State, whether a communication should not be made to the High Sheriff of Carnarvon as regards the Gaol, and to the Chairman of the Quarter Sessions as regards the House of Correction, recommending that Mr George be dismissed from their service.

He added a rider:

> It is much to be regretted that the Visiting Justices did not exercise due diligence in making themselves acquainted with the Gaol Acts, under which they are empowered to act, and with the rules of the officers of the prison as defined and regulated. If they had done so they would have seen that there is no Act of Parliament which empowers Justices to compel debtors to work at all; and they would have seen by Rule 18 of the Carnarvon Rules, under the head 'Visiting Justices', that they are to see that materials and proper implements are provided for the employment of such debtors *as may be willing to work.*

He went to great detail to delineate further discrepancies in their official behaviour. The importance of keeping daily records was emphasised.

William Henry George was duly dismissed.

Some twenty-five years later another Governor, John Dixon, was similarly charged. This charge was brought by a prisoner, Henry Gilliman, and a prison warder, Owen Jones. In his defence statement Dixon reported Gilliman to be 'very disorderly' and 'being guilty of abusive and insubordinate language'.

A month later, a 'memorial' signed by 195 ratepayers and other residents in the town accused John Dixon of 'Gross wanton and systematic cruelty towards the prisoners under charge', and demanded an enquiry. A later charge of drunkenness was added to the list made against Dixon.

The case rumbled on for several months, the Governor and the prisoner and warder concerned adding fuel to the fire until finally, in May 1869, John Dixon was given six months' notice to leave his post.

September 1869 saw an advertisement in the press:

> WANTED, a Governor of the County Gaol of Carnarvon, salary £150 a year and gas, to understand and be able to speak the language will be a recommendation.

He was expected to be responsible to the Sheriff for the proper discharge of his duties. In the following weeks around thirty applications from a wide area flowed in to the office of the Clerk to the Peace, some from ex-army officers or retired policemen, others from men already in the prison service elsewhere. Richard Roberts, late of Liverpool City Police and a Welshman, was chosen.

John Dixon moved to Manchester and was given a small pension from the Caernarfon county rate, but the magistrates refused to give him any testimonial after his twenty-two years at Caernarfon Gaol.

The ultimate sentence

The 18th and 19th centuries saw several executions in Caernarfon, the convicted being taken by horse and cart to the bank of the river Seiont where the gallows stood until an Act of Parliament of 1823 decreed that all executions were to take place privately within a prison precinct.

The death sentence, in early days, could be given arbitrarily for a number of crimes, some of them relatively insignificant.

In 1756 a tinker from the Conwy valley escaped transportation. He, 'Sion gŵr Marsley' (John the husband of Margery) was hunted, recaptured and taken to Caernarfon Gaol to await his trial. Found guilty, he was sentenced to death and, as legend has it, sang verses about his experience on the way to Pont Seiont, his last journey.

Two years later, two men were executed for mutiny.

The last execution at Pont Seiont took place in 1822. Lewis Owen was sentenced to death for attempting to shoot a man and stealing his horse. Fortunately, he was a poor shot, and the man was treated and recovered sufficiently to give testimony at Owen's trial. The incident had taken place on the road between Bangor and Capel Curig. Lewis Owen, a former soldier, was tracked down in Denbigh, and kept in gaol there before being transferred to Caernarfon.

The prison chaplain gave Lewis Owen his constant attention, persuading him eventually to acknowledge his crime and seek forgiveness. Owen admitted to a sinful life. The story goes that the condemned man made the journey to the scaffold sitting on his own coffin and listening to the chaplain reading from the Bible.

In those days executions were carried out in public. They drew large crowds with everyone eager to witness the final drop. Hawkers and beggars went along, so did the ballad-mongers selling their latest compositions on the sad life of the unfortunate person to be hanged.

From 1823, executions in Caernarfon took place in the Dungeon Tower of the castle, which by then was part of the Gaol. Although the public were not allowed access, they gathered outside when news of an execution was announced.

Some years passed before this actually happened in Caernarfon. In 1853 John Roberts attacked a schoolmaster, Jesse Roberts, in a wood in the Conwy valley, shot him twice and stole his victim's watch and a shilling or two. John Roberts, alias Jac Swan, was tried at Caernarfon and sentenced to death by hanging. After pressure from the prison authorities Jac Swan, too, admitted his guilt. But a complication arose when after his trial he accused William Evans, father of another applicant for the post of schoolmaster which had been given to Jesse Roberts, of having given him the gun and payment for shooting Jesse so that Evans's son should have the post. Evans was brought to Caernarfon Gaol for questioning, but the magistrates could find no case to be answered and he was allowed to go.

Before his execution was to take place, Jac Swan attempted to escape by pleading with a warder to leave him alone as he was unwell, but his attempt did not succeed. He was overpowered and returned to his cell. He finally admitted that William Evans had nothing to do with the murder. Jac Swan's execution took place on 10 August, 1853.

In 1878 Beaumaris Gaol, which housed only a few prisoners by this time, was one of a number of small prisons in the country to close. Those sentenced to imprisonment at the court in Beaumaris were then sent to Caernarfon Gaol to serve their sentences.

An Amlwch man, Thomas Jones, was the next for whom the death penalty was to be carried out in Caernarfon. In 1886, it was said, he absconded from the army to marry an Amlwch woman, but her family never accepted him as he was a common hawker and, in their opinion, not a suitable match. After two years of marriage they parted, and Thomas Jones took to travelling and hawking his goods around the country districts of northern Wales. He met a young woman from Llŷn, Mary Burton, and they lived together for nine years. Thomas drank heavily and abused Mary.

During one cold winter's night in 1897 they sought shelter in a lodging house in Ffestiniog. Thomas was already drunk. The lodging housekeeper refused him more ale, so they left with Thomas forcing Mary Burton to go with him, to head for Llanrwst. He was heard speaking roughly to her as they left.

Thomas murdered Mary on Manod mountain, then tried to cover his action with a cock-and-bull story. He claimed that Mary was his wife, and had become hysterical and that he had done all he could to stop her from killing herself but was unsuccessful. His story was discounted with the judge pointing out the nature of the wounds on Mary's body which could only have been inflicted by a murderer. Thomas had spent the night in Caernarfon Gaol before being transferred to Dolgellau for trial as the murder had taken place in Meirionnydd. After the trial he was returned to Caernarfon Gaol. His legal wife was then living in Caernarfon but did not visit him. He met his end on 3 August, 1898. His body was buried within the Gaol precinct.

The last man to be hanged at Caernarfon Gaol was William Murphy, an Irishman from Leigh in Lancashire, a labourer on the railway in Anglesey. He had married Gwen Ellen Jones of Bethesda. There were two children from her previous marriage. Murphy was working away from home for long periods and the marriage was not a success. He went home to spend Christmas 1909, and found that Gwen Ellen and the children had left. His father-in-law told him that they had gone to Anglesey to live with another man. This new situation incensed William and he vowed to find her, which he did, in Holyhead. Murphy threatened to kill her but did not do so then as the children were with her at the time, and he did not want them to witness the killing. They agreed to meet at 'The Bardsey Inn' in Holyhead on Christmas night, to discuss their relationship. On her way home from there Murphy strangled Gwen Ellen. Next day he visited her lover and confessed to the murder, even taking him to view the body.

At the trial in Beaumaris, Murphy pleaded insanity at the time of the attack, but the court chose to inflict the death penalty. A recommendation for mercy was rejected.

As he was about to be taken to the Dungeon Tower, Murphy climbed on the table in his cell and jumped down, turned to the hangman and said, 'I suppose it will only be like that'. When told it would, Murphy walked firmly to the gallows. His body, too, was buried in the Gaol precinct.

When the Gaol was adapted for council offices in 1932, the bodies of Thomas Jones and William Murphy were re-interred in unmarked graves at Llanbeblig.

Malice aforethought at Rhiw

During the 18th century the way of life in south Caernarfonshire revolved around the sea. Those who inhabited the towns and villages were involved in fishing and sailing as well as farming and vessels in and out of the small ports which dotted the coastline were the most convenient way of moving goods as land communications were poor, but they upheld the age-old traditions so far as the sea was concerned.

The inhabitants of Llŷn knew all about how the vagaries of the weather could bring tragedy. Poor as most of them were, they took every opportunity to take advantage of what storm and shipwreck could bring them.

Porth Neigwl (aptly named Hell's Mouth in English because of the ferocious storms which battered its wide beach) was the place for beach-combers following storms. Many a Llŷn cottage was enhanced by an item or two picked up after shipwreck when frail craft were split open by high seas and hurricane-force winds, and their cargoes tipped in to the sea along with ship's furnishings. These were eagerly grabbed as they were washed ashore, by those looking for treasure.

One night at the beginning of January 1742 a small merchant ship foundered in a storm off the island of Enlli (Bardsey). The crew of five took to their small boat and attempted landfall. One of the crew was a Welshman, the rest were Irish. After a horrendous night of being tossed in mountainous seas, when they thought their death by drowning was inevitable, they landed on the beach at Porth Neigwl. The captain ordered one sailor, William Morgan, and a young cabin boy, Edward Halohan, to stay on the beach close to the boat, which also held some of their belongings, while he and the remainder of the crew went inland to look for shelter. The captain knew that the danger from scavengers could be imminent, and thought it wise to order the Welshman to remain behind so that he could converse with any of the local people who might appear.

The night was dark. The shipwrecked crew had managed to keep a lantern alight in the boat, and this had been sighted from the shore by men on the look-out for possible jetsam. They hurried down to the shore and found William Morgan and Edward Halohan guarding the boat, a chest of cutlery and some blankets. Without compunction one of them stabbed Morgan to death, and the boy was suffocated. They made off with their spoils, to bury them so that nobody else would find them. But what of the bodies?

The captain and his other crew members arrived at Plas yn Rhiw where they received shelter for the night. The following morning the owner sent a servant to the beach to learn the fate of Morgan and the boy. He found two Rhiw men there, John Roberts and Huw Bedward, standing over the boat and the two corpses. It later transpired that John Roberts was trying to persuade Huw Bedward to help him bury the bodies before anyone found out about the murders.

The corpses were taken to St Aelrhiw's church nearby where they were buried the following day. It was claimed they had met their death through drowning. But not everyone was satisfied that that was so, and three days later the bodies were exhumed for the Coroner to carry out his examination. The injuries were still apparent, and he confirmed that they had been murdered.

The rector's too-prompt Christian burial service was queried by some, who later expressed the view that he had been in collusion with the murderers. But eventually he was exonerated.

Then began the task of finding who was to blame. John Roberts and Huw Bedward, two labourers at Rhiw, the men found at the scene the morning after the storm, were the obvious suspects and they were taken by one of the Caernarfon castle constables into custody at Caernarfon, to await their trial before a Justice of the Peace at Quarter Sessions, who then referred them to the Assizes.

This involved a waiting time of some months as prisoners, during which time they had to be fed and maintained through the generosity of friends and family as no such attention was available at the Gaol in those days.

Roberts and Bedward duly appeared before Judge Thomas Martyn and a jury of fourteen at the Assizes.

The case could not have been strange to Judge Martyn as he had previously sat at Beaumaris Assizes to hear the case of the Crigyll Robbers, a band of thieves who tempted unwary ships to the shore on wild nights by 'Cornish Lamping', tying lamps to cattle moving on the fields fringing the shore and then stealing the wrecked cargoes. Judge Martyn was remembered at the Beaumaris court and thereafter throughout northern Wales for being drunk and incapable at the time of the trial, which, in the event, ended with the defendants being released as they had found a keen barrister to represent them, and friends arrived at the Beaumaris court to create a stir and threaten the jury. There were no such scenes at Caernarfon, however.

The official verdict upon John Roberts read:

The jurors for our sovereign Lord the King upon his oath present that John Roberts late of the parish of Rhiw in the county of Carnarvon Labourer not having the fear of God before his eyes, but being moved and ordered by the justification of the Devil in the night time of the sixth day of January in the sixteenth year of the King our Sovereign Lord George the second now King of Great Britain and Ireland and so forth with force and arm at the Parish of Rhiw aforesaid in the County aforesaid and in and upon William Morgan in the peace of God and of our said Lord the King feloniously, wilfully and of malice aforethought did make an assault and that the said John Roberts with a certain knife with the value of sixpence which he the said John Roberts in his right hand then and there had and held the said William Morgan into and upon the nape of his neck then and there feloniously, wilfully and of malice aforethought . . . did kill and murder against the peace of our said Lord King his Crown and Dignity.

Then the brief endorsement:

Guilty, to hang, Judge Thomas Martyn.

Huw Bedward was accused of suffocating the boy, found guilty, and the same sentence was passed. The sentences were carried out within two weeks of the trial.

Did the sorry events at Porth Neigwl make any difference to the attitude of local people at Rhiw towards beach-combing following a storm? It is doubtful, but it was said in their mitigation that villagers referred to the tragedy with shame for many years afterwards.

A colourful prison character

Even today, every prison has its characters, whether convicted or awaiting trial. Some are perpetual offenders whose lives are spent in periods of imprisonment in various gaols around the country, depending on where their crimes have been committed.

One such was John Jones, nicknamed 'Coch Bach y Bala', whose legendary escapades became known to many of the prison authorities in northern Wales and beyond. He had over ten convictions for theft and breaking and entering. He held the police in contempt. On one occasion he rioted against them in Bala. Once in gaol, however, he proved to be a model inmate except for one or two instances of attempted gaol-break, one of them at Caernarfon gaol.

John Jones worked in a number of occupations – as a bricklayer, a joiner, a labourer. He spent a period at sea as a stoker. His thieving was no underhand business for he appeared to be proud of his ability, boasting of his exploits to anybody who cared to listen. He had a mania for collecting all kinds of items, many of them worthless. No man was safe when John Jones was around.

As time passed this eccentric thief became known for his impudent attempts at escape from gaol, which were to earn for him the added sobriquet of 'The Welsh Houdini'.

His first escape, in 1879, took place at Ruthin prison where he was serving a sentence for stealing watches. One evening, when the staff were at supper, he succeeded in opening his own cell door and three others, and walking out of the gaol. He remained free for three months before being found, and returned to prison.

His second gaol-break happened in Caernarfon Gaol in 1900, where he was lodged temporarily before being transferred to maximum security at Dartmoor. He had been convicted for theft at Beaumaris, but by that time Beaumaris gaol had been closed and those found guilty at Beaumaris court were incarcerated at Caernarfon. This time he was not so fortunate. Although he had barricaded his cell door, and begun to tunnel through the floor, his plan failed and his sentence was lengthened. Dartmoor proved invincible. Following a trial on a charge of burglary and assaulting a 71-year old woman in 1906 he was again convicted to seven years' imprisonment. He conducted his own defence at the trial, keeping the magistrates from their beds until three o'clock in the morning as he made his long speech.

The Governor of Caernarfon Gaol had cause to remember Coch Bach y Bala.

A prisoner released

It was 1843. Ann Rogers of Bangor Street, Caernarfon, had given birth to a daughter, Ellin Emily, nine weeks previously, a sister for Mary Jane who was a year and seven months old. John Rogers, the children's father, was a man of some means who could afford to keep servants and part of whose responsibility was to care for the children.

The practice of administering gin to a fractious child was common. On September 30 Ann Rogers had instructed one of the servants to buy three pennyworth of gin from the druggist, but the servant, believing she knew better, sent a young servant to the shop to buy 'a pennyworth of laudanum'. This was on a Saturday evening which was a busy time for the druggist and she was given the laudanum in an unmarked bottle. She returned with it to the house.

The children who, in the words of the servant, 'were cross', were given the drug undiluted. Both babies died the following morning. A doctor had been called but he was unable to save either child. In his evidence at the inquest the doctor told the Coroner how he had been called to the children: 'The servants said that they had not given either the syrup of poppies or laudanum to the children, in fact nothing but gin and water. From the symptoms observed on the younger child I infer the cause of death to have been the administration of some preparation of opium or other narcotic,' he said.

The servant was arrested and kept in Caernarfon Gaol from October 1843 until the next Assizes in March the following year.

A report of the trial appeared in an issue of the *Caernarfon &
Denbigh Herald*:

The judge stated, by an interpreter to the poor woman that
although he had no doubt of her innocence as far as motive was
concerned, yet the verdict of the jury (guilty) was a correct one,
for that servants and nurses were not to be permitted
ignorantly to trifle with the lives of children who might be
committed to their care. He was willing to give full credit to her
previous good character and trusted the sad results of her folly
would be a warning to her in future. It was necessary that such
conduct as hers should be severely punished but, as she had
been already kept in confinement for a long time, the Court
would only further detain her until the conclusion of the
Assizes.

Mary Jane and Ellin Emily are buried in the churchyard at
Llanfair-is-gaer. Their grave is marked with the inscription:

Beneath this stone are lowly laid
Two lovely babes as ever breathed.
They poisoned were and from their mother torn,
Both liv'd and died the very same morn.

The Eagle Tower and the Welsh Dragon

During the 1930s nationalistic feeling in Wales was beginning to run high, and all kinds of means were sought to publicise the growing claim that the Welsh language should receive its rightful place in Welsh life, and that Wales should be recognised as a nation.

Early in 1932 the government was requested to allow the Welsh flag, the red dragon on its green and white background, to be flown side by side with the Union Jack on the Eagle Tower of Caernarfon castle to commemorate St David's Day. The request was refused.

This refusal was sufficient to light a fuse among the nationalists and four (two solicitors among them) raided the castle on March 1st and removed the Union Jack flying on the Eagle Tower, replacing it with the Red Dragon. When the exchange was noticed officials promptly removed the Welsh flag and replaced this with another Union flag. One of the raiders was held in Caernarfon Gaol for the day.

News of the attempt travelled fast and by lunchtime on the same day a group of students at the University in Bangor came to hear of it. They hired a lorry from a sympathetic builder and drove post haste to Caernarfon where they entered the castle legitimately, paying the entrance fee, crossed the lawn and made for the Eagle Tower. Uninterrupted, they took down the Union flag and ran down to the lawn where they joined hands and sang the Welsh national anthem.

By this time a crowd had collected outside on 'Y Maes' ready to welcome the jubilant raiders. The Union flag was ripped into pieces, each student keeping one piece as a memento. The police were there too, but made no attempt to arrest anyone.

After the celebratory cheers the students walked to the bus to take them back to college, but on the way they were accosted by police who took their names and addresses.

But – did sympathies run high? Nothing more was heard of the incident, neither from the police nor from the University authorities.

Now the Welsh flag flies freely from the top of the Eagle Tower.

Protest and action end in court

During the 1930s Welsh nationalism made the headlines once again. There were many protests at the stubborn attitude of the then British government in refusing to acknowledge the Welsh as a nation apart. Plaid Cymru, the National Party of Wales, was gaining popularity and fought hard, through vociferous protests against what they believed to be injustice towards recognising the language and traditions of the Welsh way of life.

A bête-noir was the use of Welsh resources without consultation.

As events in Europe were threatening conflict, the government planned an airfield where servicemen in the Royal Air Force would learn the techniques of accurate bombing from the air. The first choice was an area in England, but local protest was so strong that this was abandoned and they turned their attention to Penyberth, farmland in the Llŷn peninsula close to the wide, curving bay of Porth Neigwl. As soon as the news spread, protests were voiced from many local organisations and individuals who believed it would be sacrilege to use an area of great natural beauty for such a purpose. And, the fact that this was being done without prior consultation – in other words, a blatant take-over contrary to local wishes – only added fuel to the protest.

The Caernarfonshire branch of Plaid Cymru was one of the first groups to protest, but to no avail. It seemed as though the beautiful sandy beach at Porth Neigwl was fated to be the practice ground of student bombers.

The St David's Day conference of Plaid Cymru was loud in

condemnation. One speaker, university lecturer Saunders Lewis, promised the conference 'we object to this villainy in every way. We shall fight to prevent it, and in doing so, destroy it.'

Work on the site began when wooden huts were built for the workmen. This was the spur for action.

Secretly, plans were set in motion by Plaid Cymru members. A group of seven decided that action was needed where words had failed, and they would set out to prevent any further development. With the support of four who prepared access to the site under cover of darkness and helped to carry inflammable materials, three advanced on the huts and set fire to them, beating a hasty retreat as the fire spread. The conflagration was seen over miles of the Llŷn peninsula.

The three arsonists, Saunders Lewis, Lewis Valentine and D. J. Williams, went immediately to the police station in Pwllheli to report their action to a surprised officer and to give their reasons for taking it. The following day all three appeared before the local magistrate who passed the case on to the court in Caernarfon, where the men appeared on 18 September, 1936. Such was the interest that a large crowd congregated outside the court, singing and chanting, and leaflets prepared by Saunders Lewis and Lewis Valentine were distributed among the crowd.

The political importance of the case was recognised by the Bench, and the trial was put forward to January 1937, to be held at the Old Bailey in London. The perpetrators were given sentences of nine months' imprisonment. They were proud of their efforts, and the publicity they created for the cause.

The courts today

Over the last half century there have been changes in the way justice is administered. Petty Sessions have given way to the Magistrates' Court which has taken over many of the responsibilities of the Quarter Sessions, long since disappeared. Crown Court now hears serious indictments, and the term Assize has passed into history.

Today, defendants can be tried summarily by the Magistrates or, if their charge is serious, by judge and jury at Crown Court. It has been estimated that only some three per cent of cases go to Crown Court.

The calendar for 2006 at Caernarfon Crown Court reflects life in the twenty-first century – abuse by vandals which caused an elderly man to retaliate tragically with his shot gun; a murder of an elderly woman by her husband; a hit and run traffic accident; a death caused by a site accident when an unqualified driver operated a digger; a woman who caused the death of a cyclist; a farmer who had not fed his stock sufficiently, so causing deaths among the animals; a voyeur university student who had filmed without consent. And so it goes on, with each new century bringing its problems to court.

A Magistrate can pass sentences of up to six months' imprisonment. Since late 2006 Magistrates are allowed to imprison for up to a year in a second or third charge, which obviates the case going to Crown Court.

Crown Court at Caernarfon is at present one of those on the Chester circuit, but this will change in 2007 when it becomes one on the all-encompassing Wales circuit.

Further reading

Lewis Lloyd: *The Port of Caernarfon*

W. H. Jones: *Old Caernarfon*

T. Meirion Hughes: *The Black Cap and Flag*

John Davies: *A History of Wales*

A. D. Carr: *Medieval Anglesey* (for the framework of the administration of law and order in medieval times)

Calendar of Quarter Sessions Records at Gwynedd County Record Office, Caernarfon

W. Ogwen Williams: *Caernarfonshire Historical Society Transactions,* Vol. 10 (for review of the changes which took place following the Statute of Wales 1535)

O. M. Roberts: *Oddeutu'r Tân* (the story of the arson at Penyberth)

R. Gwilym Hughes: *Dŵr dan y bont* (the Eagle Tower event)

By the same author:

   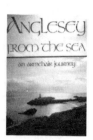

£4.50   £4.50   £4.50   £4.50

 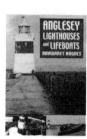  

£4.95   £4.95

£3.95   £4.75

£5.50

£14.50

All published by Gwasg Carreg Gwalch